ROBERT MANGOLD

Professional Use Only.
Wear Respirator and Gloves.
Take Maximum Precautions.
jaune foncé
dunkelgeel
donkergeel
Diane Townsend Artists' Pastels
SOFT FORM
385 Broome St.
New York, New York, 10013
Since 1971
REMBRANDT
artists' pastels
640.9
Diane Townsend Artists' Pastels
TERRAGES
385 Broome St.,
New York, New York, 10013
Since 1971
REMBRANDT
artists' pastels

ROBERT MANGOLD

Drawings and works on paper 1965–2008

March 6–April 4, 2009

PACEWILDENSTEIN

32 EAST 57TH STREET NEW YORK NY 10022

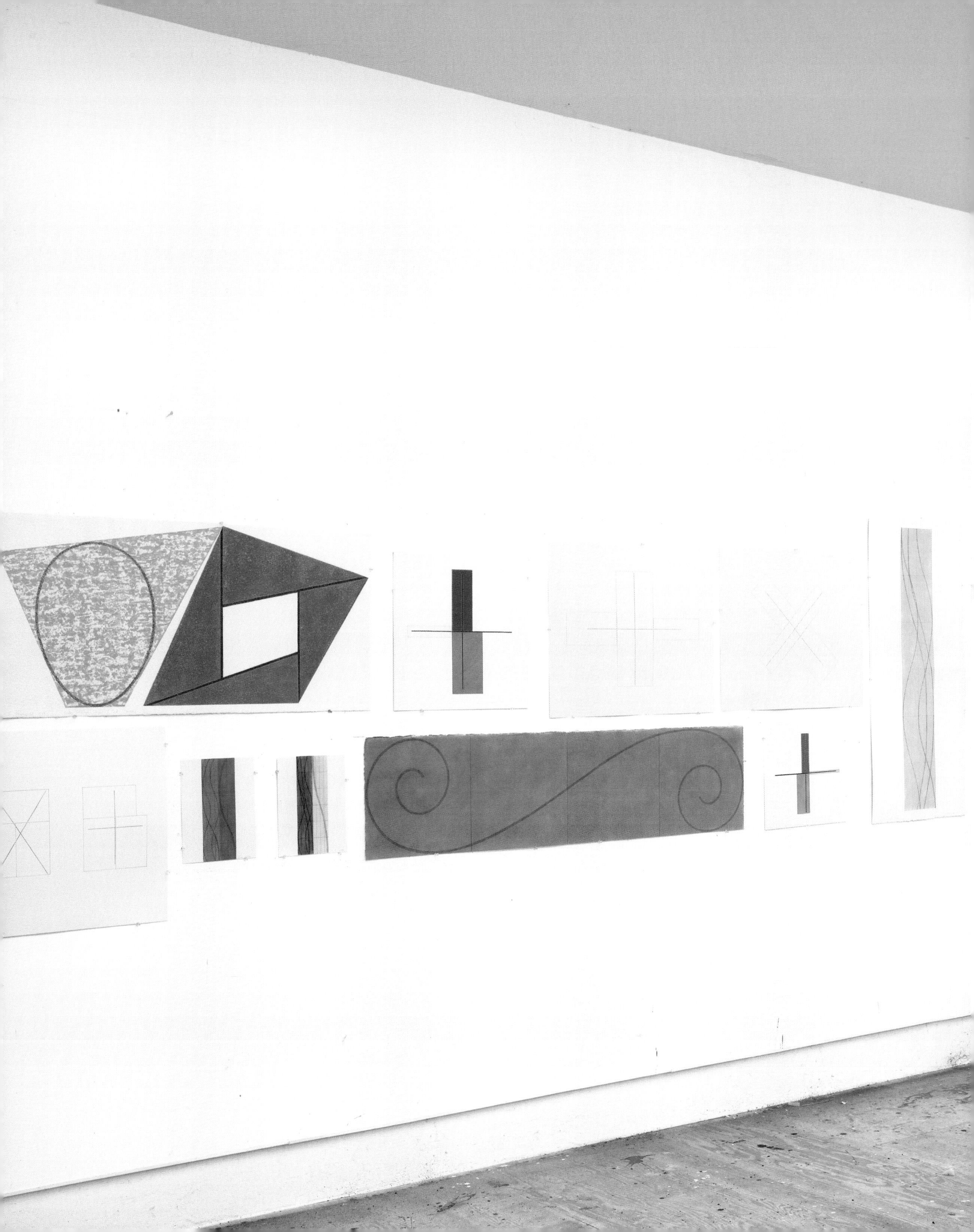

Wall-Eyed

Nowadays it is common for people to organize their thoughts according to what is displayed on their computer "desktop." Of course, that term is a misnomer, since it is the whirring machine itself that sits on the top of one's desk and the screen that rises vertically from it. This linguistic substitution is a signal of the industry's awareness that in its struggle to adapt to new technologies, the general public prefers the reassurance that old usages afford. Indeed, people persist in such habits even when everything else associated with what academic post-modernists might solemnly call the "site of 'écriture' "—that's French for "writing" and I do it just for fun—has disappeared into boxed circuitry, flickering screens, and chattering plastic keys, with paper, pens, and pencils being the primary casualties.

Nevertheless a preoccupation with "layout," which was formerly the province of the graphic artists' guild, has become that of pretty much everybody who does anything electronically. Consequently, when engaging in my own "écriture" and addressing it to the general reader, I feel safe in assuming that that person will be familiar with the routine, but also with the pleasure of opening up files, sorting icons—I further assume that the reader is visual and therefore favors pictographs over lists—and making patterns on their "desktop." The act of opening files that have for a greater or lesser period contained data generated and then occulted in a previous moment has the effect of jolting one into fresh consciousness of earlier, half-forgotten states of mind, while adding to this insight an air of mystery that accompanies the realization that one is the archaeologist of one's own intellect and imagination.

The patterning part is the most important, though, since it engenders new thoughts by means of a kind of cut-and-paste/point-and-click dialectics of physical juxtaposition and reclassification and mental synthesis of stored information. Under these circumstances, products of different moments reveal unnoticed or unsuspected similarities and differences. They may even go on to suggest entirely new possibilities. Thus the search for documents, the culling and reordering of files, and the resulting rearrangement of the desktop becomes the emblem of thinking itself; a game of simultaneous retrospection and projection into the future; the recombinant picture of a process.

Familiarity with that process should help those approaching Robert Mangold's recent inventory and reconsideration of his archive of drawings by bridging the gap separating the visual artist from the visual lay person because Mangold's manifest fascination with his own handiwork—that is, with things he knows better than anyone yet must relearn by rehandling—is equivalent to contemporary techno-Everyman-and-woman's experience of rebooting their brain by scanning and reordering their databank. For Mangold has effectively been performing the same operations when rolling out the drawers of his flat files, shuffling the glassine sleeves within them, extracting one or another from the stack and then extracting the drawing itself from the slippery transparent envelope and then pinning the work to the wall that runs down one side of his studio.

Where they landed on that wall—as evidenced by photographs of the installation the artist made—defies the logic of art historically linear development. Instead, their disposition seems to accent sharp contrasts and subtle correspondences, as if the readily apparent themes and variations Mangold has worked with over the years were suddenly allowed to interrupt and intersect each other like overlapping components of a larger orchestral work whose shifting dynamics and timbres were gathering toward a symphonic crescendo that is nonetheless tantalizingly deferred by the unexpected introduction of new instruments, new themes, and new sounds.

So it is that small studies for the one-, two-, three-, and four-color cruciform panel paintings of the early 1980s—a moment when Mangold responded to the brash, bright painterliness of Neo-Expressionism with his own limpid polychromy—roughly bracket a long, scrolling monochrome red ocher composition of the early 2000s, even as an asymmetrically angular diptych of the late 1980s seems to lean toward the cruciform study to the right, while the vertical wave-patterned drawing in yellow to the right of the other cruciform study picks up and attenuates the coiling curvature of the scroll drawing (pp. 4–5). Next to the yellow vertical sits a pale beige form resembling a lopsided shield or the profile of a elegantly misshapen urn, within which is inscribed a pair of triangles that push outward against the contour of the silhouetted form, as if to rationalize that disequilibrium though in actuality their exact equivalence accents the uneven distribution of space on either side of the axes they share. As anomalous as the outline of this form is in relation to that of the equilateral yellow rectangle next to it, its bowed sides nevertheless catch the undulation within the yellow field, like the sympathetic vibrations of a stringed instrument resonating in response to another, and transmit them to the even more insistently symmetrical blue ring hovering to its right on the wall above. Within the circular channel of that ring, further undulations occur and are in turn picked up by two smaller rings next to it and by the arcing shapes and ellipses that animate the drawings that continue along the expanse of the wall leading to the artist's working table.

I have chosen a narrative mode for describing the visual interaction among these works because one truly does get the sense that a continuous motion is unfolding across them, a kind of graphic chain reaction whose immediacy supersedes awareness of the discontinuity of the individual drawing's production over time. If it is not too much of a stretch, one might even compare this impression to the domino effect driving the antic, quasi-accidental narrative of Peter Fischl and David Weiss's un-still-life film *The Way Things Go* (1987). Yet there is nothing Rube Goldberg-like about the assembly of the works in Mangold's wall montage, nor about the pictorial construction of the individual drawings. Quite the contrary, they are juxtaposed with the greatest sensitivity to their internal and external configurations and threaded together with utmost grace, as if all the linear elements of the ensemble were somehow spun from the same filament.

It is at this point that the desktop-to-wall analogy breaks down, as analogies inevitably do. In our digital world it is relatively easy to "program" shapes, and plug in colors from a Pantone palette. So easy in fact that those with a designer's orientation may wonder why painters still do it the hard way. But as information engineers will tell you, not only are the marvels of the electronic age qualified by the first rule of data processing—garbage in/garbage out—but even the most exquisite nuances of machined visuality cannot escape the constraints of the particular generation of machinery in use. Since the beginning of computer technology and for the time being at least, one of the chief limitations of the medium has been the grid upon which all digital images are based.

A simple test of what this means is available to anyone who makes full use of the "zoom" function of their computer, or at any rate of the kind of specialized computers on which designers and architects plot their images. Take the electronic "pencil" with which images are drawn, and at the conventionally low resolution of the screen one can make a plausibly smooth circle, ellipse, arc, or spiral of any variety one wishes. Blow that same digital drawing up by fifty percent and the flowing line one has inscribed in electrodes becomes noticeably jagged as a result of the almost hidden mathematical compromises computers necessarily make. For given that the only options for approximating a true curve are to fill in alternating spaces closest to the mark on either the vertical, horizontal, or diagonal axes of the screen grid, all curvilinear geometries are effectively "squared off" in translation. Blow the same drawing up further and a fractal "coast line" emerges, with ever-sharper angles eclipsing the illusion of a smooth bending of forms as the enlargement proceeds. No matter how much fractal magic is performed to reduce the visibility of these angles by decreasing their scale in relation to the scale of the final image-product, even the inattentive viewer will subliminally feel their presence, which is why the animations of Pixar studios and other wizard workshops always exude an uncanny falseness—which, expertly stylized, is part of their allure—and why these technologies have yet to encroach on the territory of painters and draftsmen who persist in drawing curves without the assistance—or resistance—of gizmos which have become standard equipment in other fields.

Mangold is preeminent among those who choose to do it the hard way—by hand. However he does not fetishize touch in the manner of expressionists and others who make the artist the overt or covert subject of their work by stressing their emotional and physical presence at its creation. Nor does he foreground the difficulty of the task he assigns himself or ever let the exertions it requires show in the final work in order to highlight his virtuosity. In this he follows the example of Henri Matisse, who wrote: "I have always tried to hide my own efforts and wished my work to have the lightness of a springtime which never lets anyone suspect the labor it has cost."[1] And, undeniably, there is an evergreen freshness to the way Mangold handles the constants or near constants of his art; all those scoring, looping lines and emphatically plain but eccentrically offset polygons, all those bemusing complications of constructivist or minimalist abstractions masquerading as their radical simplification.

In the intimate format of drawing one can sense the first excitement of discovering the power of that plainness and the disorienting but enlivening effects of such calculated displacement. A few early examples straightforwardly evince the wide-open possibilities of Mangold's pictorial prestidigitation and why those digits are fingers rather than fractals. In four beautifully spare sheets from 1965 (pp. 10–11), the artist set down four variations on a deceptively reductive but in reality manifold shape. With red pencil, Mangold first delineates two "squares" that have been divided down the center, taking care to crop the lower right-hand edge, while even more assiduously making sure that the bias of that cut is more acute in one than in the other, thereby determining that it reaches almost to the central divide in the first, but only two-thirds of the way in the second. Each is a self-sufficient entity, yet the pair of them seems to tease one another into action, as if the cropped panels were moving against the flat background like opening and closing doors. They are not, of course. No illusionism is intended. Nevertheless the plane of the page flexes slightly in response to the obliqueness of the slice Mangold has taken, and flexes more as one notices the difference between the two.

In a pair of drawings dating from 1972 (pp. 12–13), Mangold chooses yet other extensions of the cut, though they are less pronounced in their differences, and then takes a right-angled chunk off the left side of his basic shape, on the bottom corner of one and the side of the other. These notches turn a somewhat deviant polygon into a memorably odd, emblematic visual object. In the same vein, Mangold ran changes on the near congruence but ultimate incongruence between curved and angular shapes, which incidentally demonstrate the inherent distinctions between fractal geometries in use on digital desktops and those available to him on a drafting table. Made from the same materials, the first is a subtly bloated circle surrounded by an irregular hexagon, the second a semicircle completed by half of a twelve-sided polygon (or an opened hexagon). These mismatched shapes are finely rendered in a way that makes their alignment or fusion almost cohesive, but never entirely so. Phrased in the period language of formalist abstraction when they were made, they are Gestalt-like but not Gestalts.

That would seem to have been Mangold's purpose. To unsettle the certainties of constructivism and its derivatives while aiming squarely—or off-squarely as the case may be—at the holism to which it aspired. In short, Mangold has not only messed with the geometries programmed into technology but with the programmatic thinking that directed New York School formalism in its heyday. Within the camp of artists who, for lack of a better term, we call Minimalist, Mangold has consistently pursued inconsistencies in order to engender new visual events that could never have been worked out like corollary equations from the axioms of postwar geometric abstraction. They had to be invented. The expansiveness of the liberties he now takes when tinkering with those inventions are obvious from his drawings of 2006 to the present, though there is nothing obvious or predictable about the contours those in rectilinear formats assume or the paths laid out by his pencil as it explore such zigzagging templates or the wide-band circles he has concentrated on most recently. Four circular drawings of 2007–08 (pp. 34–37) make the accumulating, swerving rhythms of Mangold's work of the last several years palpable. Wobbling sine and cosine curves and fractured parabolas swell within the inner and outer margins of Mangold's perforated discs, gently but surely pressuring the already taut form and, in the process, just as gently and just as surely destabilizing it, so that it rocks within the square of the white ground on which it has been circumscribed or, in cutout versions, pinioned.

In drawings, that rocking affects our internal gyroscope through the eyes. Realized on the scale of Mangold's painting, the implicit kinetics of the work would trigger responses throughout the viewer's body as peripheral vision kicks in and the vertical posture of that viewer is called into question by the disequilibrium of the composition facing him or her. However, discussion of that issue is for another occasion, although in passing it bears saying that insofar as the artist's body is the primary tool for enlarging these images, the flow of the lines we follow and the density of background tints we see—hues and tones that are individually mixed and impossible to find in the color charts used by computer-ruled graphics designers—means that bigger versions of these drawings will never just be dilated copies of an fixed prototype but will necessarily be redeployments and reinterpretations of an elastic concept. For the present, our concern is the works on paper in which the first glimmer of those concepts appeared; and glimmer and glow they do.

Robert Storr, 2009

NOTES:

1. Henri Matisse in a 1948 letter to Henry Clifford, Director of the Philadelphia Museum of Art, in Herschel B. Chipp, *Theories of Modern Art* (Berkeley: University of California Press, 1984), p. 140.

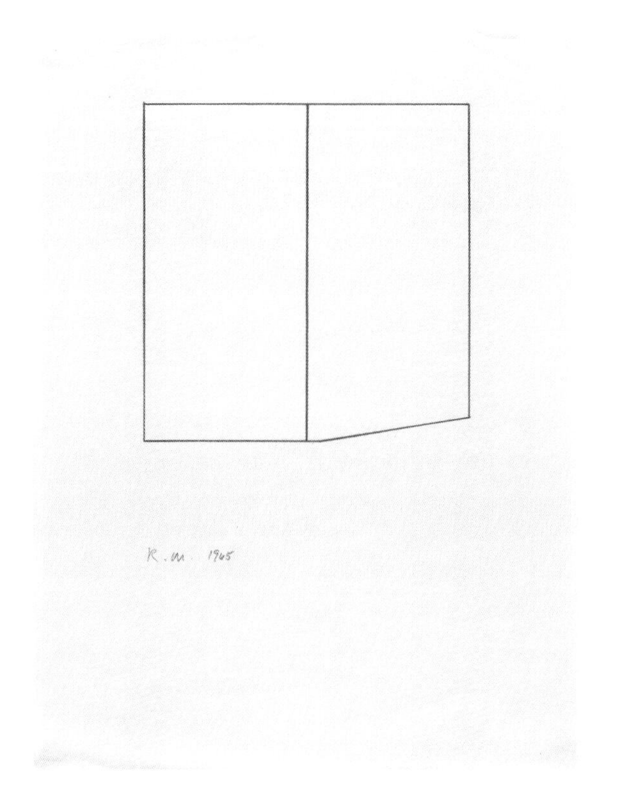

Study 1965, colored pencil and pencil on yellow paper, 11 x 8 3/8"

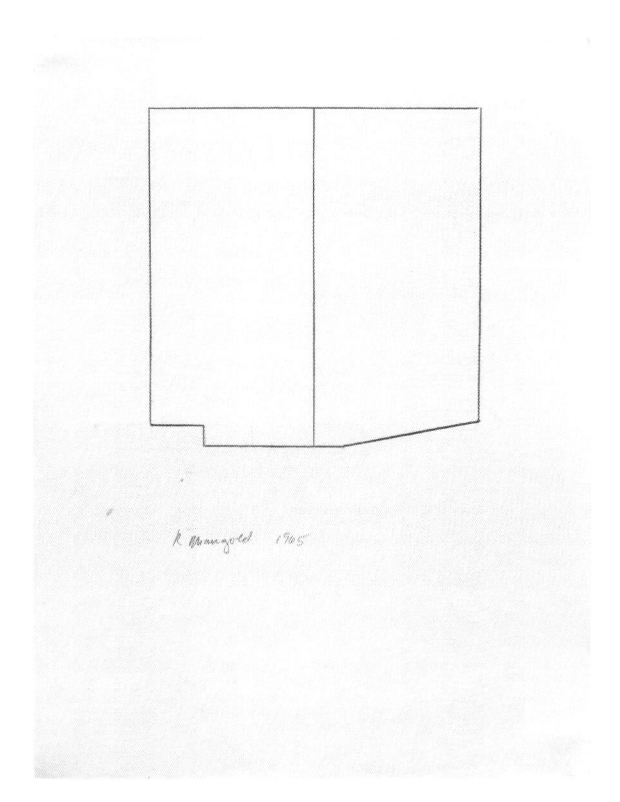

Study 1965, colored pencil and pencil on yellow paper, 11 x 8 3/8"

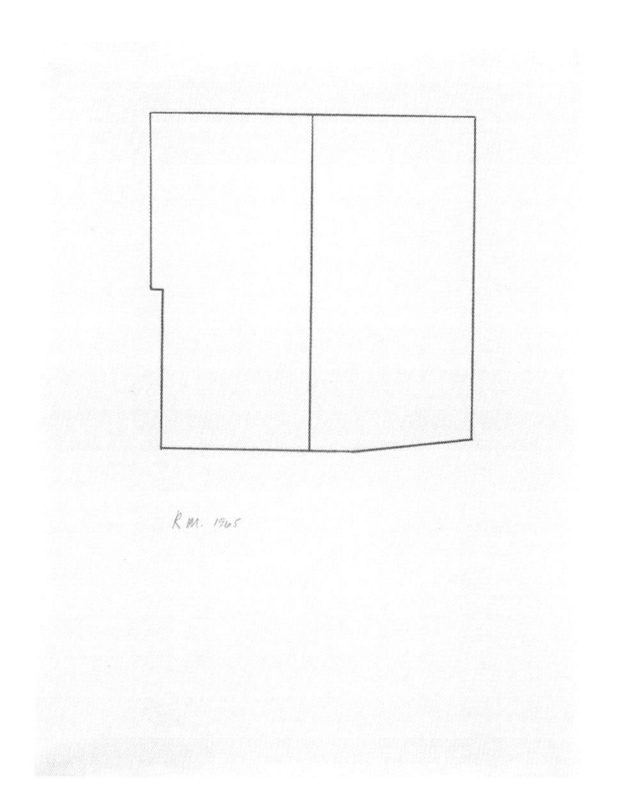

Study 1965, colored pencil and pencil on yellow paper, 11 x 8 ⅜"

Study 1965, colored pencil and pencil on yellow paper, 11 x 8 ⅜"

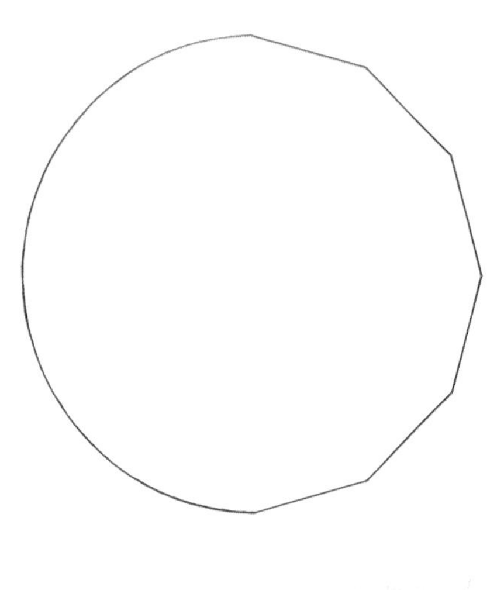

Untitled 1972, pencil on paper, 11 x 11 ½"

Untitled 1972, pencil on paper, 23 ⅛ x 29"

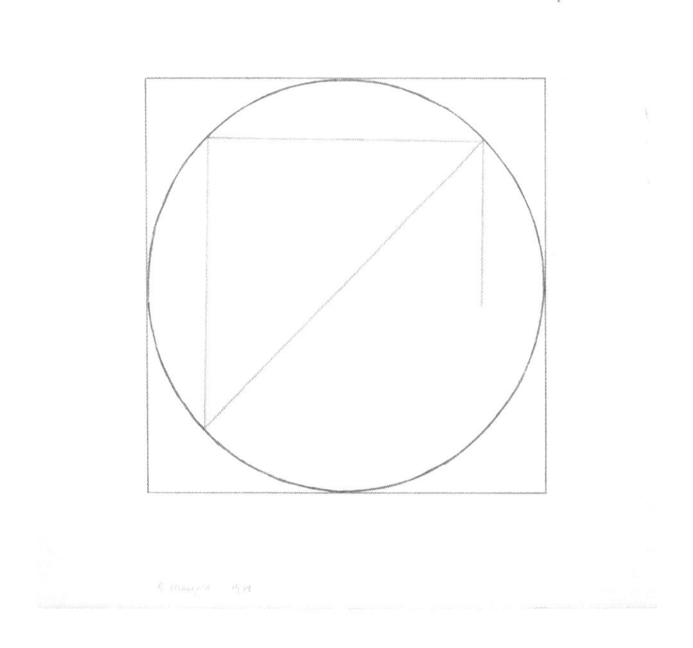

Untitled 1974, colored pencil and pencil on paper, 14 x 14"

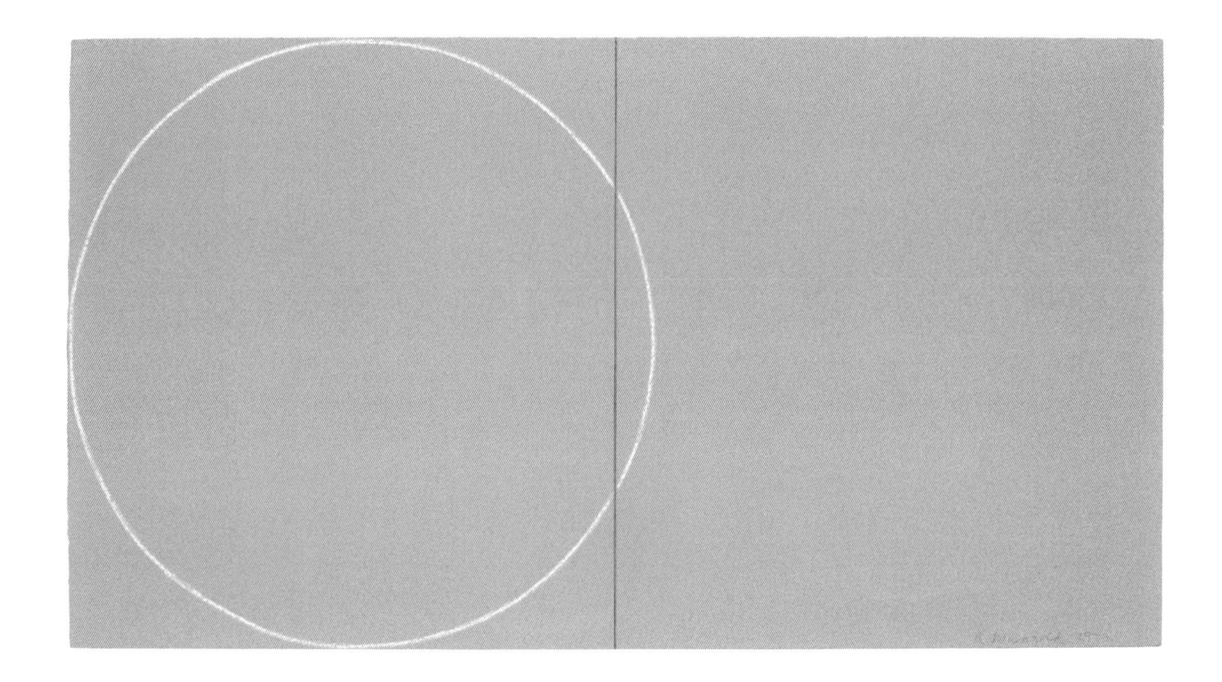

A Circle Within Two Squares 1973, acrylic, pencil and white pencil on paper, 11 ¾ x 22"

A Triangle Within Two Rectangles (Red) 1977, acrylic and black pencil on paper, 39 ½ x 55 ½"

Four Distorted Rectangles with Line Division (Green, Blue, Sand, Ocher) 1979
acrylic and black pencil on paper, 4 panels, 39 x 27 ½" each
The Museum of Modern Art, New York. The Judith Rothschild Foundation Contemporary Drawings Collection Gift.
Given in honor of Mrs. June Noble Larkin 2005

X Within X (Red) 1980–81, acrylic and pencil on paper, mounted on board, 10 x 11 ⅛"

X Within X (Pink) 1980–81, acrylic and pencil on paper, mounted on board, 10 x 11"

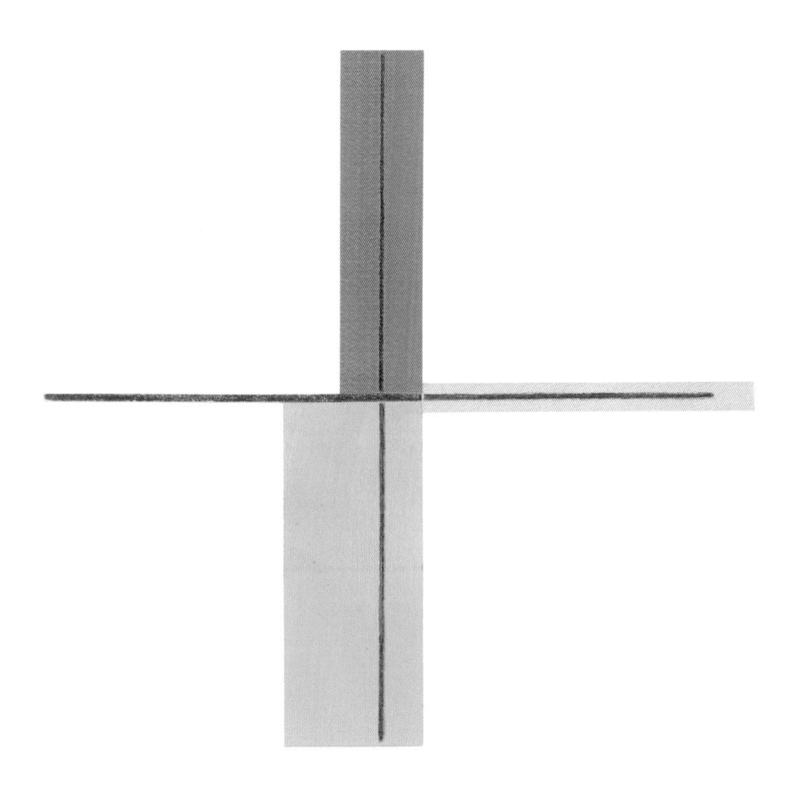

Blue-Green/Orange/Pink + Painting 1982, acrylic and pencil on paper, mounted on board, 16 x 16"

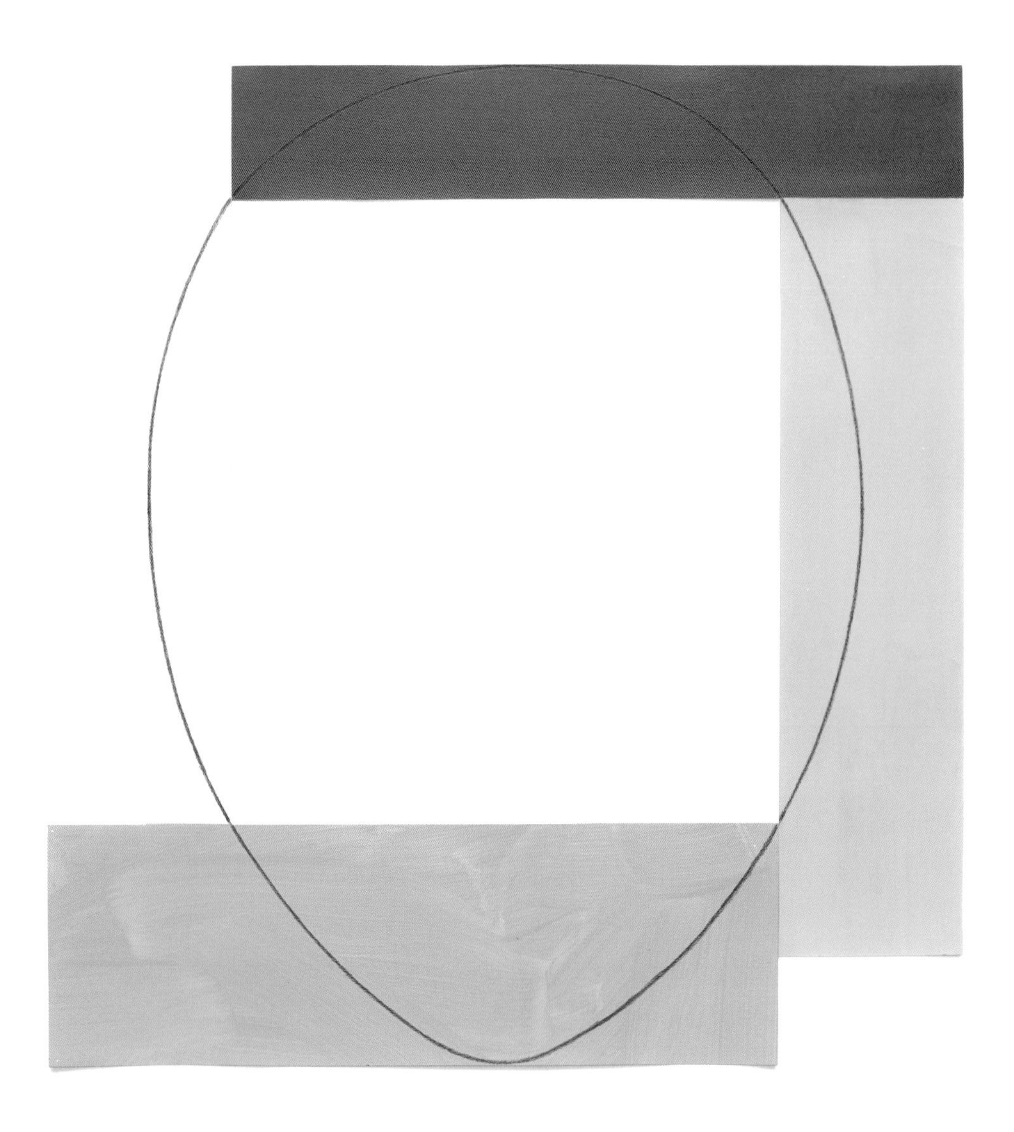

Four Color Frame Painting #1 1983, acrylic and black pencil on paper, 37 x 35"

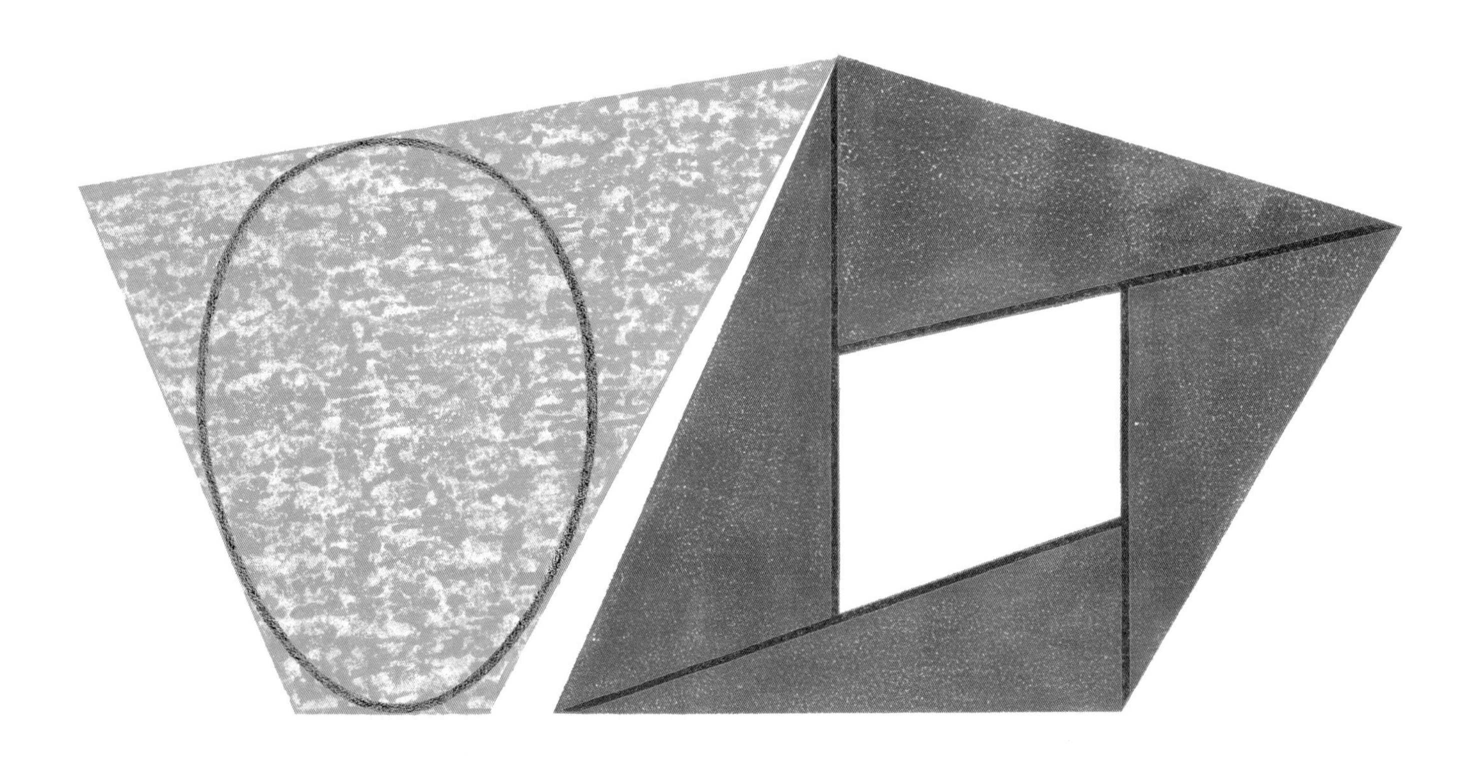

Yellow Orange Ellipse/Red Frame 1988, acrylic and black pencil on paper, 22 ⅜ x 44 ⅜"

Study Attic Series X 1990, acrylic and black pencil on paper, 30 x 22"

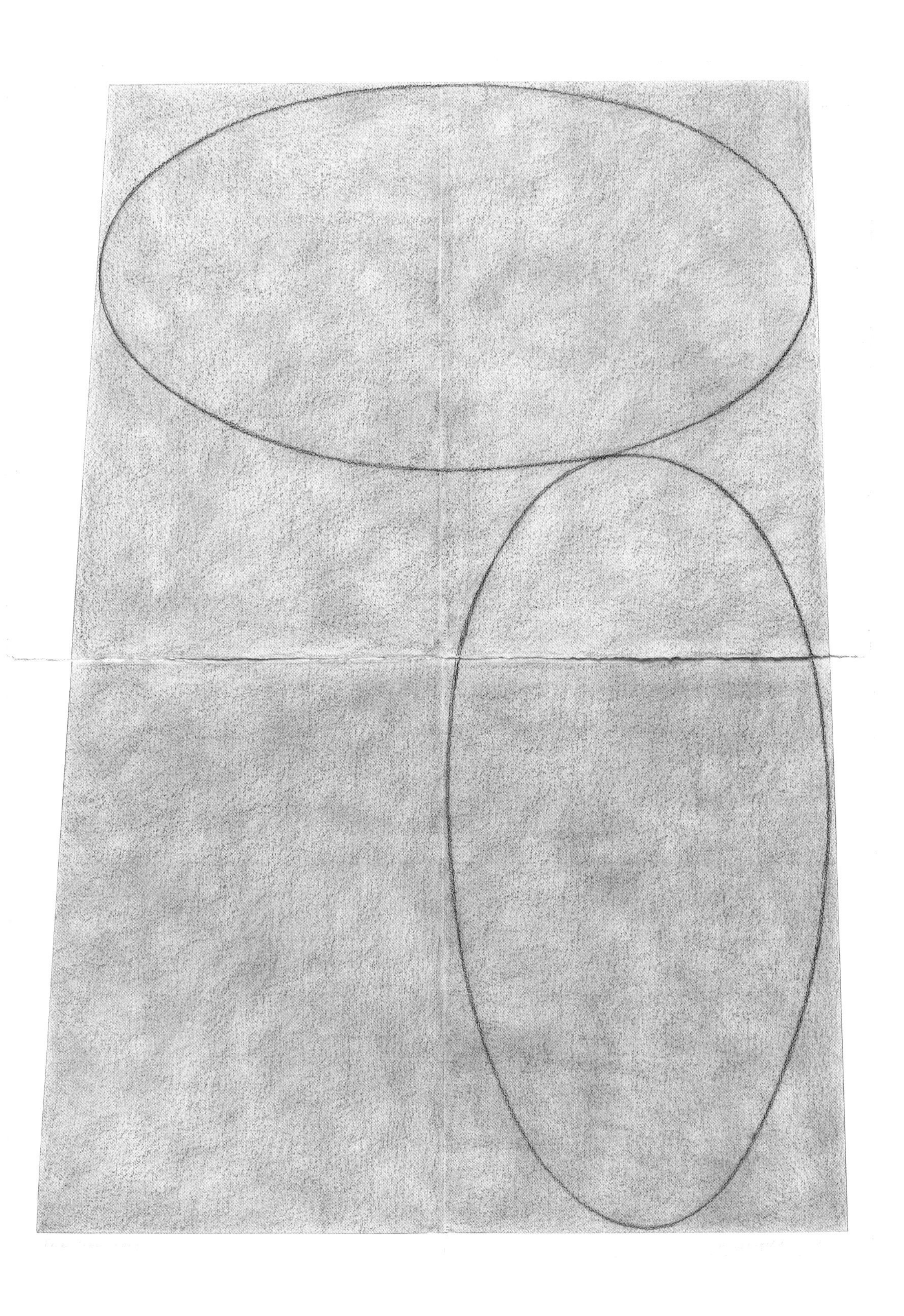

Plane/Figure Drawing 1992, graphite and black pencil on paper, 2 panels, 30 ¼ x 45" each; 60 ½ x 45" overall installed

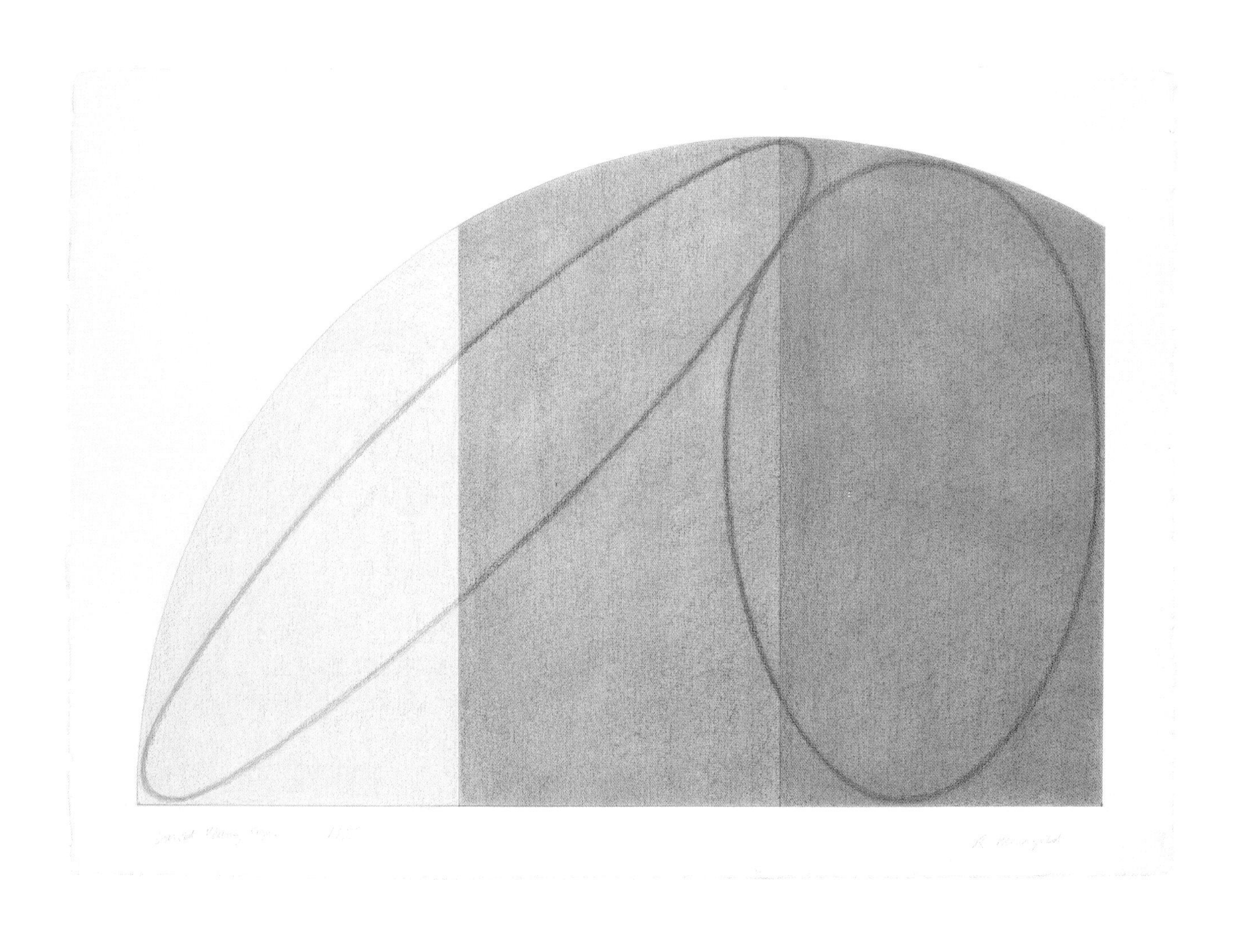

Curved Plane/Figure 1995, acrylic, graphite and black pencil on paper, 29 ¼ x 41 ¼"

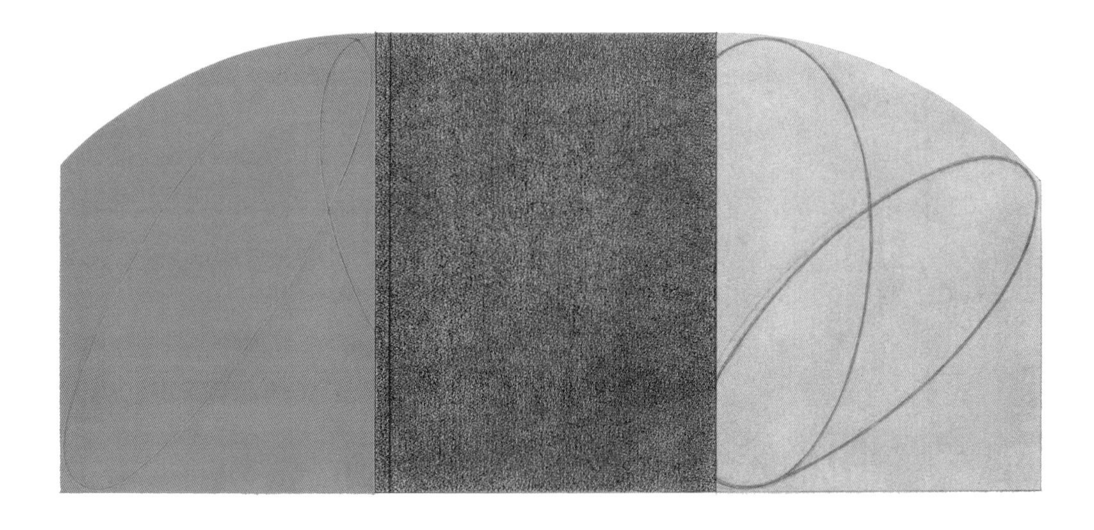

Orange/Gray Zone 1996, acrylic, graphite and black pencil on paper, 29 ½ x 41 ½"

Untitled 1999, acrylic and black pencil on paper, 41 ¼ x 29 ½"

Curled Figure 2001, acrylic and pencil on paper, 20 ½ x 40 ¾"

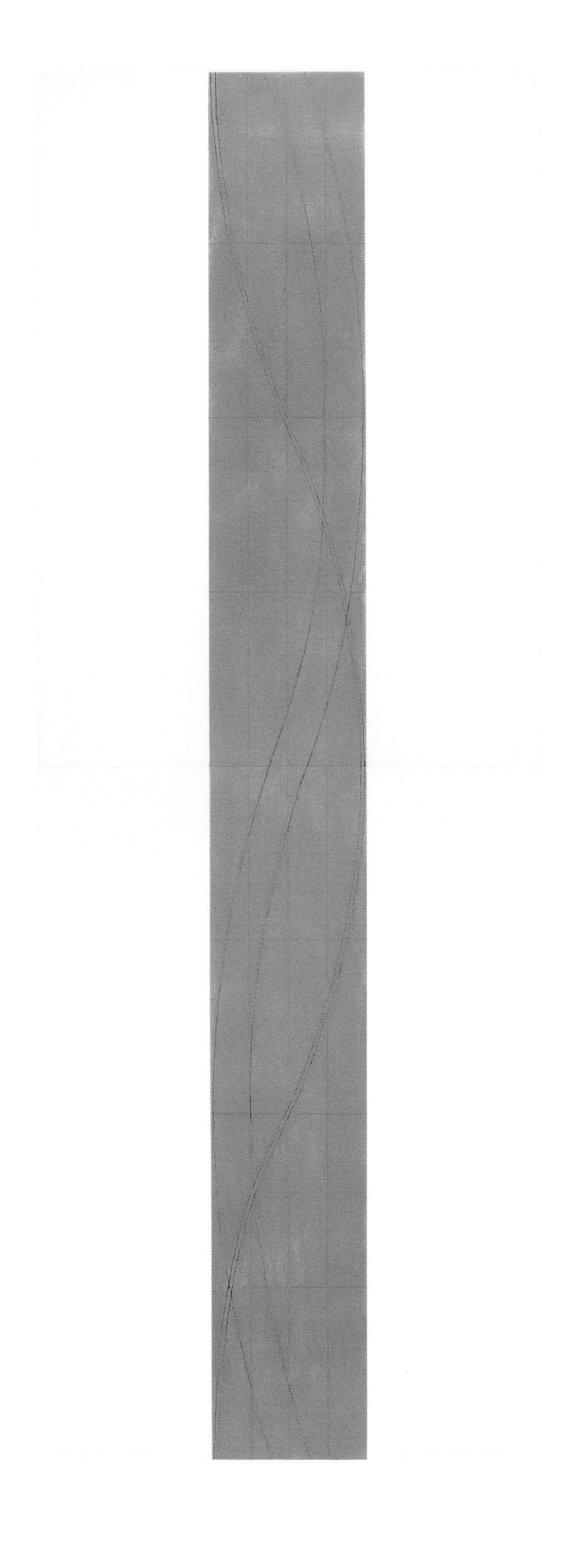

Double Line Column Study 2005, pastel and black pencil on paper, 60 ¼ x 22 ½"

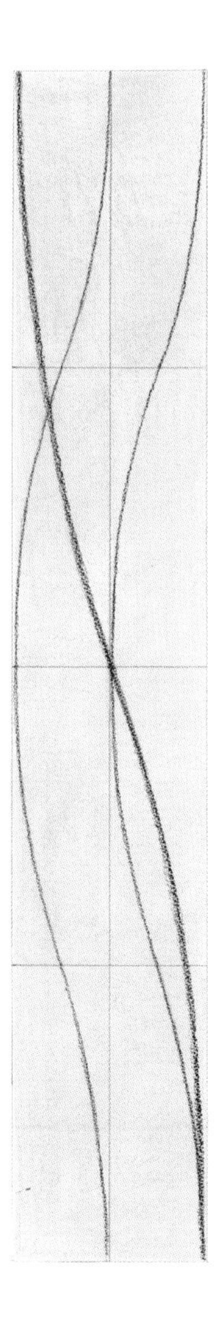

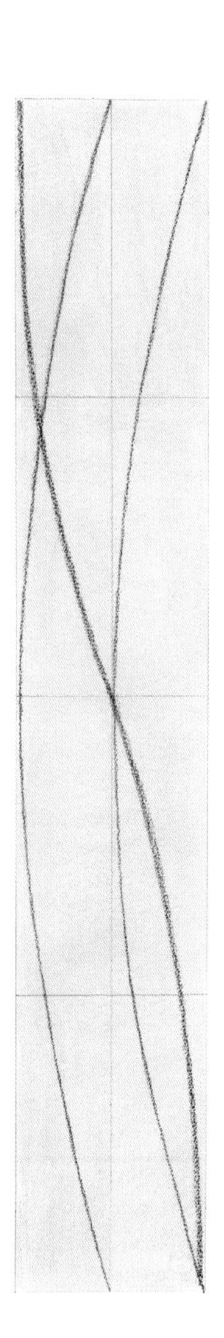

Two Columns 2006, pastel and black pencil on paper, 30 ¼ x 22 ½"

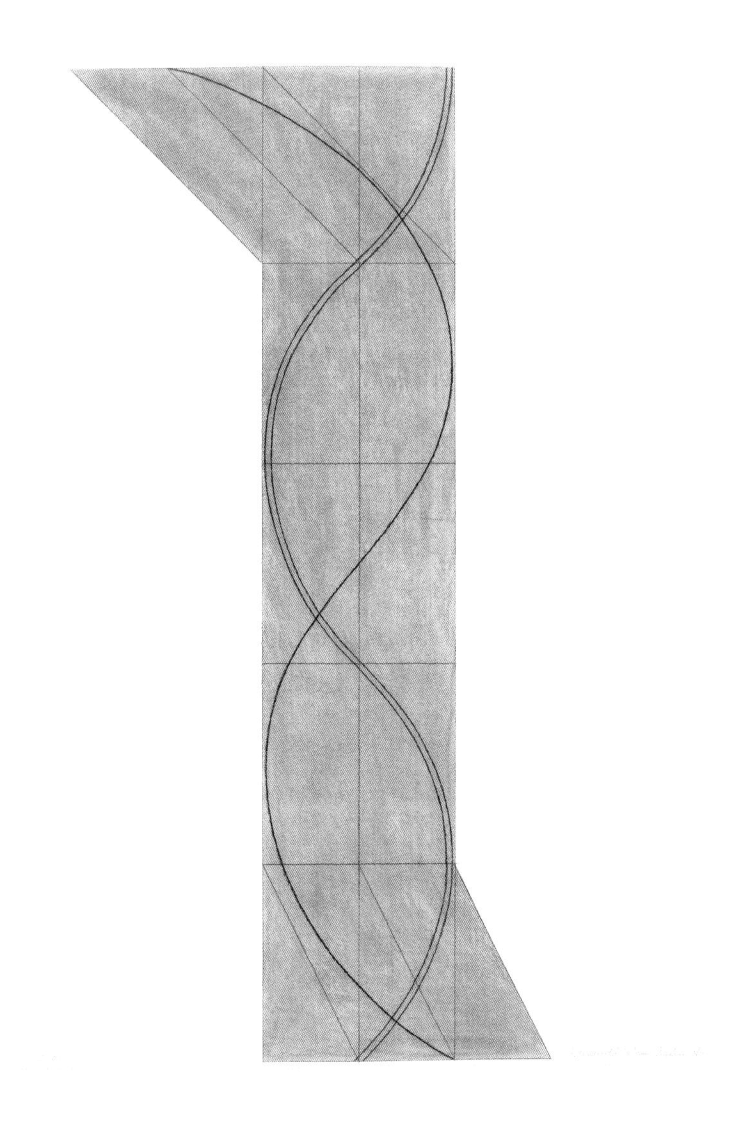

Column Structure VII 2006, pastel and black pencil on paper, 30 ¼ x 22 ½"

Column Structure XXII 2008, pastel and black pencil on paper, 30 ½ x 24 ½"

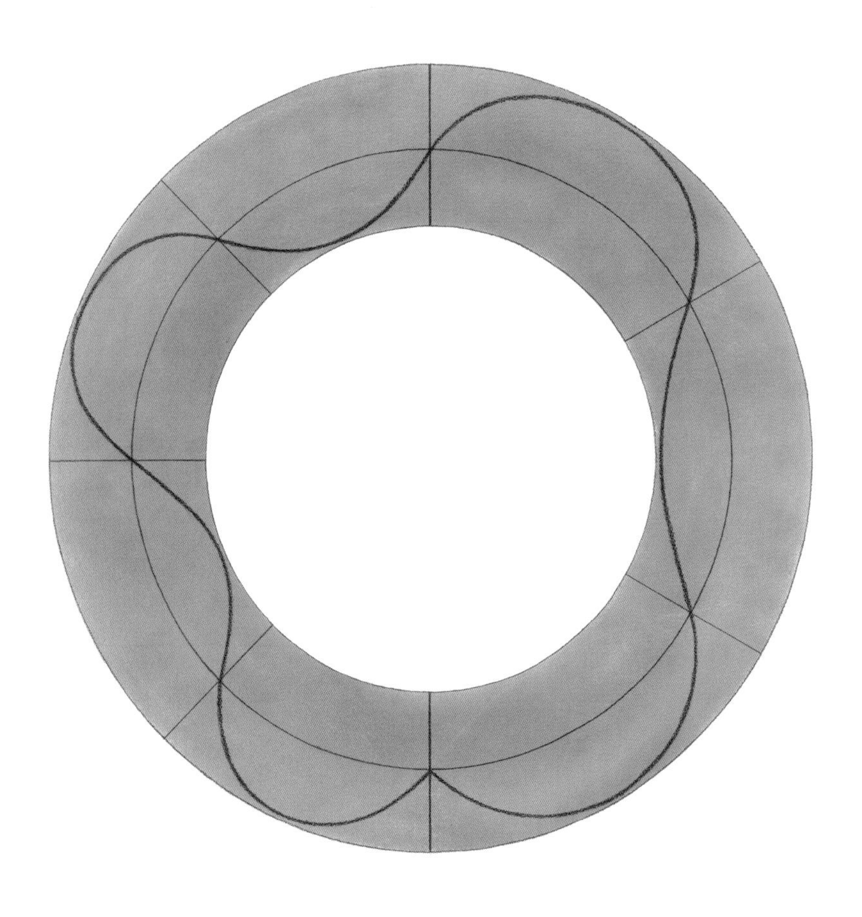

Ring Image B 2007, pastel and black pencil on paper, 31 ¼ x 29 ½"

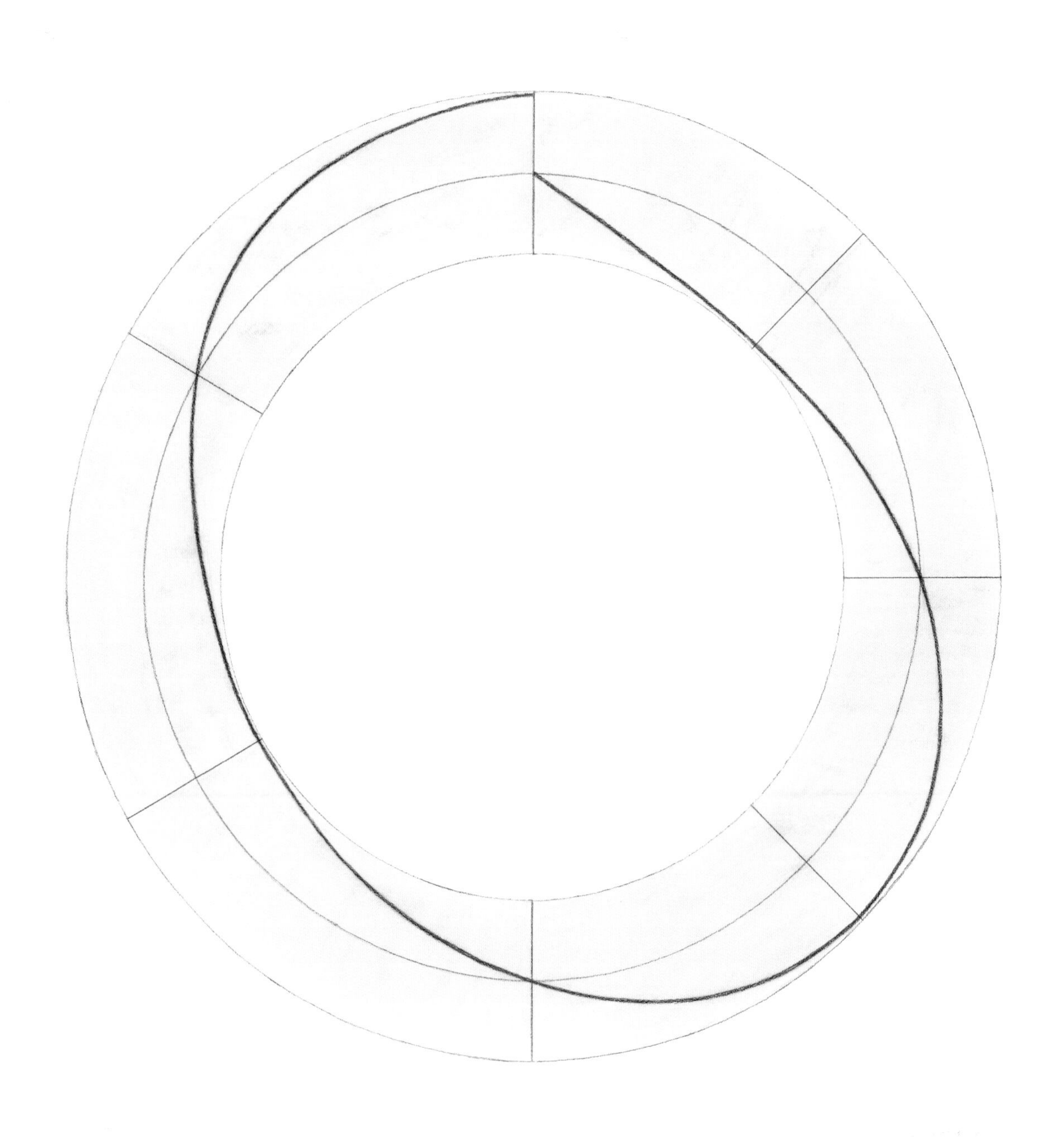

Ring Image F 2008, pastel and black pencil on paper, 41 ½ x 40 ½"

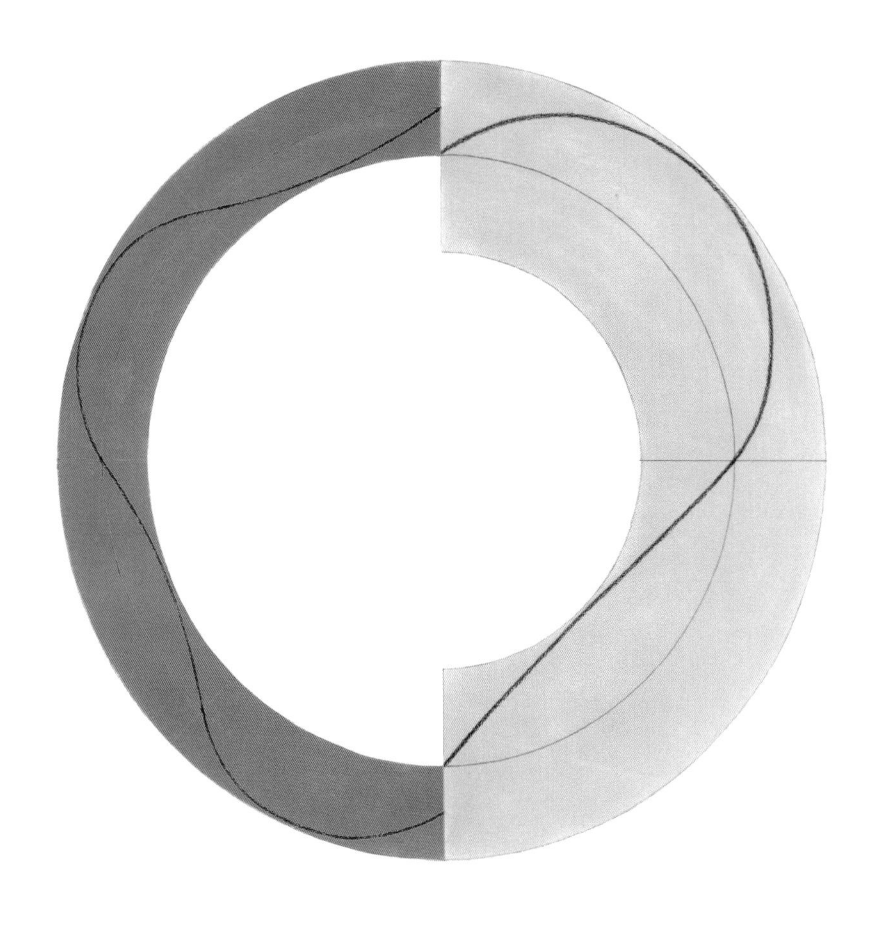

Split Ring Image B 2008, pastel and black pencil on paper, 31 ½ x 29 ½"

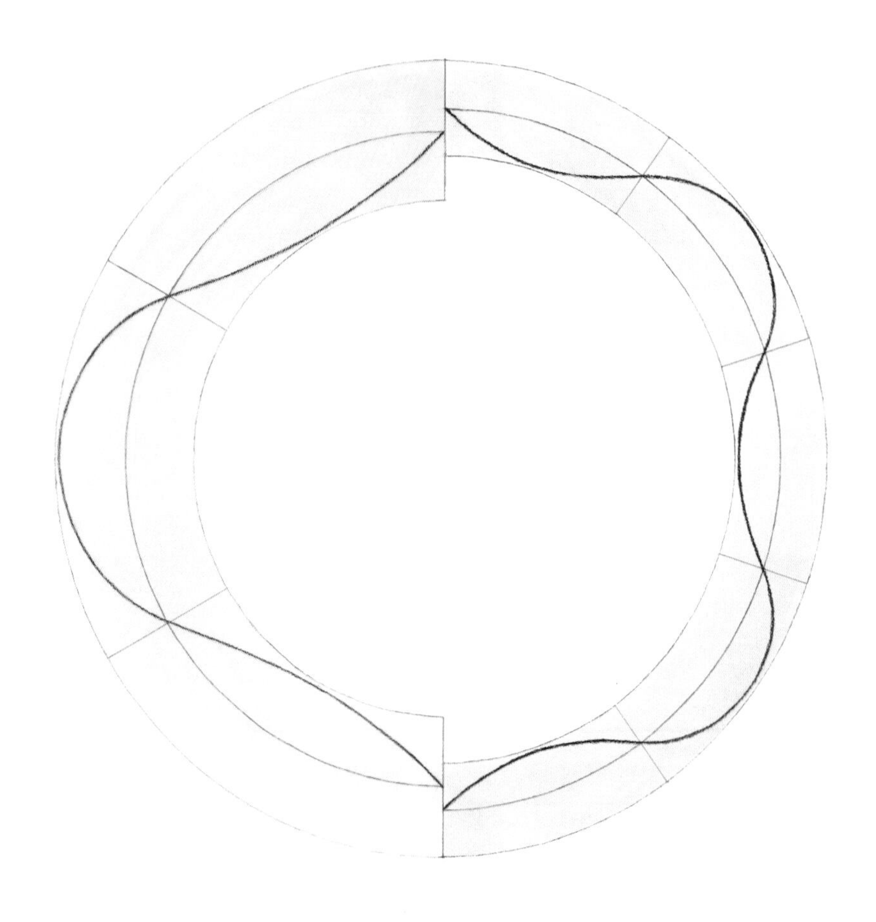

Split Ring Image 2008, pastel and black pencil on paper, 31 ½ x 29 ½"

Checklist

10

Study
1965
colored pencil and pencil on yellow paper
11 x 8 3/8"

Study
1965
colored pencil and pencil on yellow paper
11 x 8 3/8"

11

Study
1965
colored pencil and pencil on yellow paper
11 x 8 3/8"

Study
1965
colored pencil and pencil on yellow paper
11 x 8 3/8"

12

Untitled
1972
pencil on paper
11 x 11 1/2"

13

Untitled
1972
pencil on paper
23 1/8 x 29"

14

Untitled
1974
colored pencil and pencil on paper
14 x 14"

15

A Circle Within Two Squares
1973
acrylic, pencil and white pencil on paper
11 3/4 x 22"

17

A Triangle Within Two Rectangles (Red)
1977
acrylic and black pencil on paper
39 1/2 x 55 1/2"

18–19

Four Distorted Rectangles with Line Division (Green, Blue, Sand, Ocher)
1979
acrylic and black pencil on paper
4 panels, 39 x 27 1/2" each
The Museum of Modern Art, New York. The Judith Rothschild Foundation Contemporary Drawings Collection Gift. Given in honor of Mrs. June Noble Larkin 2005

20

X Within X (Red)
1980–81
acrylic and pencil on paper, mounted on board
10 x 11 1/8"

X Within X (Pink)
1980–81
acrylic and pencil on paper, mounted on board
10 x 11"

21

Blue-Green/Orange/Pink + Painting
1982
acrylic and pencil on paper, mounted on board
16 x 16"

22

Four Color Frame Painting #1
1983
acrylic and black pencil on paper
37 x 35"

23

Yellow Orange Ellipse/Red Frame
1988
acrylic and black pencil on paper
22 3/8 x 44 3/8"

24

Study Attic Series X

1990

acrylic and black pencil on paper
30 x 22"

25

Plane/Figure Drawing

1992

graphite and black pencil on paper
2 panels, 30 ¼ x 45" each;
60 ½ x 45" overall installed

26

Curved Plane/Figure

1995

acrylic, graphite and black pencil on paper
29 ¼ x 41 ¼"

27

Orange/Gray Zone

1996

acrylic, graphite and black pencil on paper
29 ½ x 41 ½"

28

Untitled

1999

acrylic and black pencil on paper
41 ¼ x 29 ½"

29

Curled Figure

2001

acrylic and pencil on paper
20 ½ x 40 ¾"

30

Double Line Column Study

2005

pastel and black pencil on paper
60 ¼ x 22 ½"

31

Two Columns

2006

pastel and black pencil on paper
30 ¼ x 22 ½"

32

Column Structure VII

2006

pastel and black pencil on paper
30 ¼ x 22 ½"

33

Column Structure XXII

2008

pastel and black pencil on paper
30 ½ x 24 ½"

34

Ring Image B

2007

pastel and black pencil on paper
31 ¼ x 29 ½"

35

Ring Image F

2008

pastel and black pencil on paper
41 ½ x 40 ½"

36

Split Ring Image B

2008

pastel and black pencil on paper
31 ½ x 29 ½"

37

Split Ring Image

2008

pastel and black pencil on paper
31 ½ x 29 ½"

Photography:
G.R. Christmas; cover, pp. 2, 4-5, 15, 21, 24, 26-31, 33
Joerg Lohse; pp. 12-14, 20 (top), 22
Kerry Ryan McFate; pp. 10-11, 17, 20 (bottom), 23, 25, 34, 36-37
Ellen Page Wilson; pp. 18-19

Design:
Tomo Makiura
Sandra Watanabe

Production:
PaceWildenstein

Color correction:
Motohiko Tokuta

Printing:
Meridian Printing, East Greenwich, Rhode Island

ISBN: 978-1-930743-98-4